WITHDRAWN

A Good Night's Sleep

By Sharon Gordon

Consultants

Nanci Vargus, Ed.D.
Primary Multiage Teacher
Decatur Township Schools, Indianapolis, Indiana

Jayne L. Waddell, R.N., M.A., L.P.C.
School Nurse/Health Educator/Lic. Professional Counselor

Children's Press®
A Division of Scholastic Inc.
New York   Toronto   London   Auckland   Sydney
Mexico City   New Delhi   Hong Kong
Danbury, Connecticut

Designer: Herman Adler Design
Photo Researcher: Caroline Anderson
The photo on the cover shows a child sleeping.

Library of Congress Cataloging-in-Publication Data

Gordon, Sharon.
  A good night's sleep / by Sharon Gordon.
      p. cm. — (Rookie read-about health)
Includes index.
Summary: Explains in simple terms why the body needs sleep, what happens
to the body during sleep, and ideas for falling sleep.
  ISBN 0-516-22570-7 (lib. bdg.)   0-516-26874-0 (pbk.)
  1. Sleep—Juvenile literature. [1. Sleep.] I. Title. II. Series.
  RA786 .G67 2002
  612.8'21—dc21
                                    2002005482

Good morning!
How did you sleep?

Everyone needs a good night's sleep. You will feel tired without it.

You might yawn a lot. You might even feel a little grumpy!

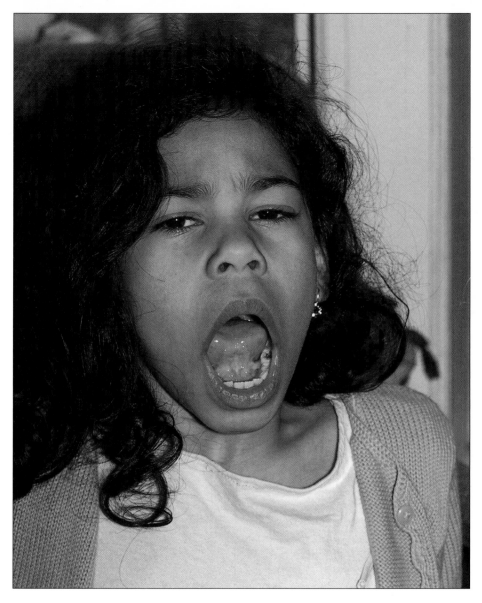

It is hard to think or learn without a good night's sleep.

Sleep gives our bodies a time to rest and grow. It keeps us from getting sick.

What happens when
you sleep?

Does everything in your
body stop? Not at all!

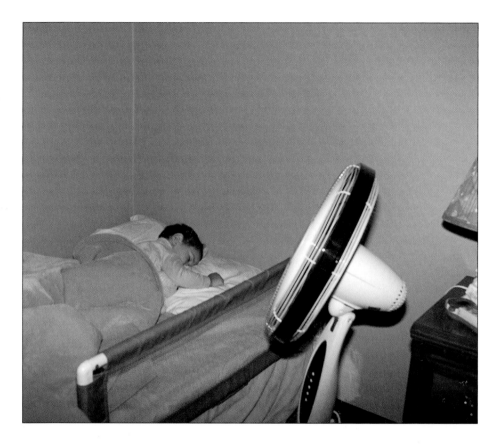

10

Your heart keeps beating.
Your lungs keep breathing.

But some things do
change when you sleep.
You will hear some things
but not others.

Your brain knows which
sounds are important.
It knows which ones are
not. Do you wake up
when you hear your
alarm clock?

13

14

Your mind begins to
dream when you sleep.

What did you dream
about last night? Can
you remember?

There are some dreams
you would like to forget
because they scare you.
They are called nightmares!

Some people can sleep
sitting up. Some people
talk in their sleep.

Some people even walk in their sleep.

Children should try to sleep at least ten to twelve hours every night. Your body is growing, so you need lots of sleep.

19

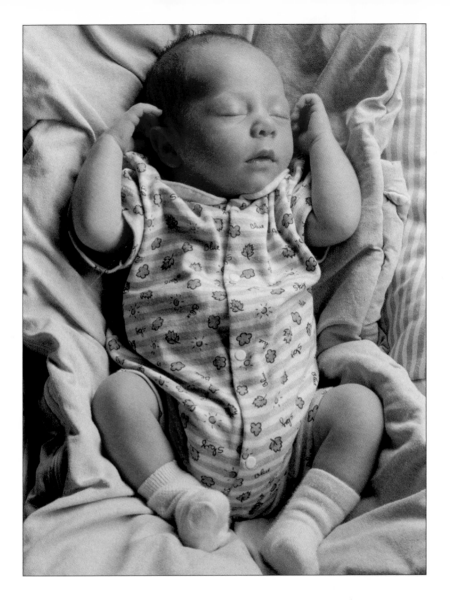

Older people might only need seven to nine hours of sleep.

A new baby sleeps more hours than it is awake!

Take a short nap during
the day if you are tired.
Don't sleep too long.
You might not be able
to fall asleep at night.

There are some things that can help you fall asleep.

Some people like to drink a glass of warm milk before bedtime.

Some people read a book.
Other people might watch
TV or listen to music.

What helps you fall asleep?

27

Good night!

Words You Know

alarm clock

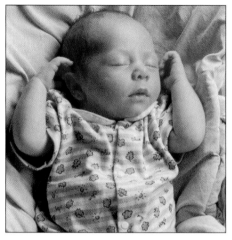

baby

growing

nap

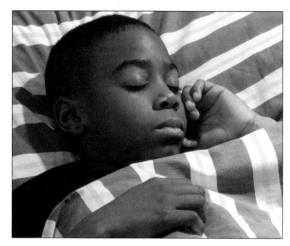

sleep

walk

warm milk

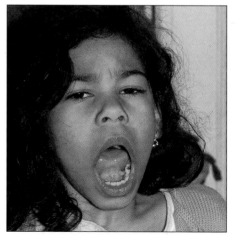

yawn

31

Index

About the Author

Sharon Gordon is a writer living in Midland Park, New Jersey. She and her husband have three school-aged children and a spoiled pooch. Together they enjoy visiting the Outer Banks of North Carolina as often as possible.

Photo Credits

Photographs © 2002: Corbis Images/Picture Press: 16; Dembinsky Photo Assoc./Gijsbert van Frankenhuyzen: 27; H. Armstrong Roberts, Inc./S. Feld: 24, 31 bottom left; ImageState/Patrick Ramsey: cover; Nance S. Trueworthy: 14; Photo Researchers, NY: 9, 31 top left (Grantpix), 3 (Richard Hutchings), 20, 30 top right (Trois JM./Explorer), 13, 30 top left (Ken Lax); PhotoEdit: 6 (Tony Freeman), 17, 31 top right (Felicia Martinez); Rigoberto Quinteros: 5, 10, 28, 31 bottom right; The Image Works: 19, 30 bottom left (Bob Daemmrich), 23, 30 bottom right (Esbin-Anderson).